# A Midsummer Night's Dream

Based on the play by
William Shakespeare

Adapted by Lesley Sims

Illustrated by
Serena Riglietti

Reading consultant: Alison Kelly
Roehampton University

# The characters

**Theseus**
(say **Thee**-see-us),
Duke of Athens,
engaged to
Hippolyta

**Hippolyta**
(say Hip-**pol**-li-ta),
Queen of the
Amazons

**Egeus**
(say E-**gee**-us),
father of Hermia,
wants her to
marry Demetrius

**Hermia**
(say **Her**-me-a),
in love with
Lysander

**Lysander**
(say Lie-**san**-der),
in love with Hermia
but enchanted to fall
in love with Helena

**Demetrius**
(say De-me-tree-us),
also in love with
Hermia and
enchanted to fall in
love with Helena

**Helena**
Hermia's best
friend, in
love with
Demetrius

**Puck**, the fairy who enchants Lysander and Demetrius

**Oberon** (say **Oh**-bur-ron), king of the fairies, married to Titania

**Titania** (say Tit-**tar**-nee-a), queen of the fairies

**Flute**, who plays Thisbe (say **Thiz**-be), a young girl in love with Pyramus

**Bottom**, who plays Pyramus (say **Pir**-ra-muss), a young man

**Peter Quince**, who is putting on a play for Theseus, the Duke

**Starveling**, who plays the Moon

**Snug**, who plays a lion

**Snout**, who plays a wall

# Contents

This book is based on a famous play by
William Shakespeare. He wrote "A Midsummer
Night's Dream" over 400 years ago, to amuse
noisy audiences. They loved mix-ups and magic
and this story is full of both.

# Chapter 1
# Wedding belles

Theseus, the Duke of Athens, was very excited. The Queen of the Amazons, Hippolyta, had agreed to marry him. Squeezing her hand, he grinned and ordered his servants to prepare for the wedding.

Soon, they were racing around the palace, polishing furniture and floors until they shone. In the kitchen, the cook began creating a cake fit for a queen.

"We shall hold the best party Athens has ever seen," Theseus promised Hippolyta.

Just then, an angry man burst into the Great Hall with three other people. "I must see Duke Theseus now!" he shouted.

"Is that you, Egeus?" asked Theseus. "Whatever's wrong?"

7

Egeus gestured at a girl in a yellow dress. "It's my daughter, Hermia," he explained. "I want her to marry this man, Demetrius."

A man in a blue tunic nodded to the Duke.

"But Hermia wants to marry Lysander," Egeus went on. "You're in charge around here. Please tell her to marry Demetrius."

Theseus frowned at Hermia. "Demetrius is a good man," he pointed out, "and the law says daughters must obey their fathers."

At this, Lysander began to plead with the Duke.

Hermia doesn't love Demetrius, she loves me. Let me marry her.

Theseus looked at the young man and shook his head. "Lysander!" he said sternly. "I'm sorry, but Hermia must marry Demetrius. It's what her father wants. If she won't do as Egeus tells her, she'll have to become a nun."

Lysander watched in fury as
Theseus left, taking Egeus and
Demetrius with him.

Hermia was dismayed. "I can't
marry Demetrius," she cried. "And
I won't be a nun."

Don't cry. We'll
leave Athens.

"I'll meet you in the forest
tonight and we'll run away," said
Lysander, trying to comfort her.

11

"Run away?" said a sad voice, interrupting them. "Who's running away?" It was Hermia's best friend, Helena. Quickly, Lysander told her their problem.

Helena sighed. "I wish Demetrius loved me the way you love Hermia."

"Poor Helena," said Lysander. "We do too. But we can't hang around," he went on. "Come on, Hermia, we must pack."

"We're leaving Athens tonight," Hermia whispered on her way out.

Left alone, Helena felt tears pricking her eyes. "It's so unfair!" she thought.

Demetrius loved me before he met Hermia.

Around her, the palace was full of noisy wedding preparations. The bustle made Helena feel worse.

"I'll tell Demetrius that Hermia is running away," she decided. "Perhaps then he'll choose me."

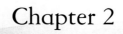

# Chapter 2

# Putting on a play

Over at the house of Peter Quince, a craftsman, things were almost as noisy. He had decided to put on a play for the Duke's wedding and asked five of his friends to help.

14

"The play I've chosen," Quince announced, "is the sad, sad story of Pyramus and Thisbe."

Bottom wasn't listening. "Oh good," he said. "I like a comedy. Who am I?"

"You'll be Pyramus," Quince told him. "A young man in love with the beautiful Thisbe."

Bottom looked pleased. "I'll make a brilliant Pyramus!"

"And Flute is to be Thisbe,"
Quince went on.

Flute looked horrified. "A girl? I
can't be a girl! I'm... I'm growing
a beard," he said.

Eugh! And it
means I'll have to
kiss Bottom.

"Oh! I could
be Thisbe too,"
Bottom offered.
"I'll speak low
for the man," he
growled, "and
high for the girl,"
he finished with
a squeak.

17

"Flute is Thisbe," said Quince firmly. "He can wear a mask. Starveling is the Moon, Snout is a wall and Snug is a lion."

Bottom hopped up and down with excitement. "Oh! Let me be the lion," he cried, giving a fierce roar.

Quince jumped in surprise.
"You'd scare the audience away,"
he said.

"Here are your words," Quince
added, handing out pieces of paper.
"Learn them quickly. We'll meet
tonight in the forest to rehearse."

# Chapter 3

# A fairy fight

Later that evening, deep in the forest, Oberon – king of the fairies – was in the middle of a fight with his dazzling queen, Titania.

They were arguing over one of Titania's servants.

"You should give him to me," Oberon declared. He followed Titania as she walked through the forest, nagging her until the Queen's head ached.

I want a page to carry my cloak.

Titania turned away, her hair glowing gold in the moonlight. "Oberon, stop it," she said. "He's my page and I'm keeping him."

She waved a pale hand and four fairies appeared. "Come!" she ordered. "We're leaving."

Oberon frowned. Titania had plenty of fairies to serve her and he needed a page boy.

Grumpily, he sat on a tree stump and wondered what to do. After a moment, his face cleared. "I need help," he realized. "Where's Puck?"

Puck!

In a flash, his jester Puck hovered before him. Puck was the most mischievous fairy of all.

"I want to trick Titania," Oberon explained. "I'm going to make her fall in love with the first thing she sees, even if it's a monkey!"

Puck chuckled. "That's the best spell I ever heard!"

"But I need a magic herb," Oberon said. "Can you find it for me as quick as you can?"

I'll search around the Earth in forty minutes!

As Puck flew into the starry
night, Oberon heard voices.
Silently, he slipped behind a tree.

It was Demetrius, looking for
Hermia, with Helena close behind.
"I don't love you anymore, so stop
following me," he snapped. But
Helena couldn't leave him alone.

It makes me sick
to look at you!

It makes me sick
*not* to look at you.

Oberon gazed upon Helena with pity. "Don't be unhappy," he murmured. "Before the night is out, that man will love you."

He looked up as Puck returned, clutching the herb.

"You found it!" cried Oberon with glee. "I want you to use some of it too," he said, telling Puck of his plans for Demetrius and Helena.

26

Leaving Puck to search for Demetrius, Oberon sped off to his queen. He found her lying on a bed of violets, with her fairies singing a lullaby. The scent of herbs filled the air, sweetening their magical song.

Oberon waited for the fairies to leave before gently rubbing the magic herb on Titania's eyes.

*What you see when you awake,*
*You will for your true love take.*

Meanwhile, Puck had found a sleeping couple... but he'd made a mistake. He didn't enchant Demetrius at all. He enchanted Lysander.

# Chapter 4

# Puck's tricks

Not long after Puck cast his spell,
Demetrius and Helena came past.
Demetrius was still determined to
lose Helena.

Leaping over tangled tree roots, he raced away from her. Helena, sunk in gloom, stopped... and noticed Lysander, fast asleep. "Lysander?" she began.

Lysander awoke and gasped with delight. "Sweet Helena," he cried. "I love you!"

Helena was shocked. "You can't!" she said. "You love Hermia."

"Forget Hermia," said Lysander.

"Stop teasing," Helena snapped. "If you're going to be silly, I'm leaving." And she left.

Lysander turned to the sleeping Hermia. "Stay there for all I care," he hissed. "I'm following Helena."

When Hermia woke, a moment later, she was alone. "Lysander?" she called. "Where are you? What's happened?" Scrambling to her feet, she went to look for him.

Puck had no idea of the trouble he'd caused. He was flying deeper into the woods, looking for fun. And who should he run into but Peter Quince, rehearsing with his friends?

"A play?" Puck thought. "I think I'll watch... and maybe I'll join in!"

Bottom was worried. "This play's too scary," he said.
"Especially the lion," Snout agreed.

Bottom stepped into the middle
of a clearing and waved his arms.
"This can be our stage," he said,
and the play began.

As Puck watched, a brilliant idea
popped into his head. When
Bottom finished his speech and left
the clearing, Puck followed.

The play went on until Flute,
acting Thisbe, called for Pyramus.
   "Fair Thisbe, I'm yours!" shouted
Bottom, crashing around a bush.
   Flute took one look at him and
screamed.

A monster!

Puck had given
Bottom a donkey's head.

"What's the matter?" asked
Bottom, who didn't know about
Puck's spell.

"Help!" Flute screamed again
and everyone ran away.

"Stop teasing me!" Bottom called
after them. He began to walk up
and down, singing loudly to
himself to show he didn't care.

Bottom's awful singing woke
Titania, who took one look at his
floppy, furry ears and fell in love.

"Whose angel voice is that?" she
asked. "Sing again, O wise,
beautiful creature."

Summoning her fairies, she
told them to feed him dewberries
and sweet, ripe apricots. "And
shield his eyes from the moon with
your butterfly wings," she said.

37

Titania stroked
Bottom's velvety nose.
"I'll take good care of you,"
she promised, kissing his
fuzzy cheek.

Puck peeked through
some leaves at them and
giggled. Springing up, he flew
off to tell Oberon of his trick.

39

# Chapter 5

# Who loves who?

"A donkey? That's better than I'd
hoped," said Oberon in delight.
Just then, they heard a shout.
Hermia, who was still looking for
Lysander, had found Demetrius.

"Did you enchant him as I asked?" Oberon whispered to Puck.

"That man? Oh no, it wasn't him," Puck replied carelessly.

Hermia and Demetrius were arguing loudly.

You must have killed Lysander! He'd never leave me.

Hermia stormed off. Demetrius shrugged. "She's crazy," he thought. "I'll wait here until she's calmed down." He sat down and yawned. Soon, he was sound asleep.

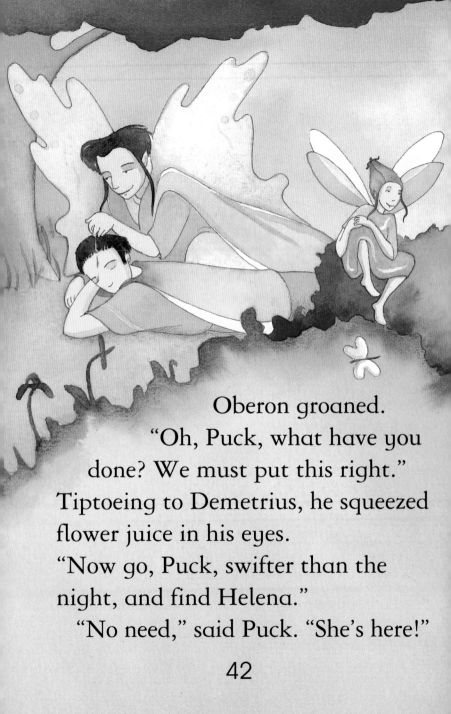

Oberon groaned.

"Oh, Puck, what have you done? We must put this right." Tiptoeing to Demetrius, he squeezed flower juice in his eyes.

"Now go, Puck, swifter than the night, and find Helena."

"No need," said Puck. "She's here!"

Sure enough, there was Helena, closely followed by a desperate Lysander. "I'm not teasing you," he insisted. "I love you!"

"Ha!" snorted Helena. "You should be saying that to Hermia."

Lysander shook his head. "I made a mistake. Besides, Demetrius loves Hermia now. He'll never love you."

"Helena, I love you!" Demetrius cried, waking up and seeing her.

Don't be unkind, Demetrius. You love Hermia.

You can keep Hermia. I love Helena.

Helena groaned. "Stop it! Stop it! Now you're both teasing me."

"Look, Lysander," Demetrius added, as he spotted Hermia. "Here comes your love now."

Hermia made straight for Lysander. "Why did you leave me?" she begged.

Helena was furious. How could her best friend be so mean? "You, you puppet!" she yelled at Hermia.

"Puppet?" thought Hermia. "She's making fun of my height." Hermia glared at Lysander. "Do you love Helena because she's taller than me?"

I'm tall enough to scratch your eyes out!

Oberon sighed. Things were getting worse. Demetrius and Lysander decided to fight each other for Helena. Both swore they loved her most.

"You'd better follow them,"
Oberon told Puck. "Keep them
apart until you've cured Lysander.
Meanwhile, I'll find Titania."

"Be quick," said Puck as he flew
away. "It's almost dawn."

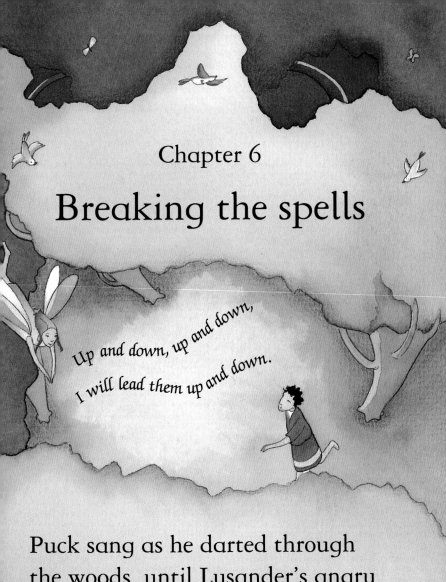

# Chapter 6

# Breaking the spells

*Up and down, up and down,*
*I will lead them up and down.*

Puck sang as he darted through
the woods, until Lysander's angry
voice interrupted him.

"Where are you, Demetrius?"

49

"Here I am!" called Puck,
copying Demetrius's voice.

Lysander ran off in the direction
of the voice, as Demetrius came by.

"Where are you, Lysander, you
coward?" bellowed Demetrius.

"Over here!" cried Puck,
wheeling around and
sending Demetrius
the opposite way.

Soon, the pair were chasing all over the forest, trying to find each other. Finally, exhausted, they lay down either side of a bush and slept.

No sooner had they fallen asleep than Helena came along. Feeling miserable and tired, she sat down without even noticing them.

Only three?
Come one more,
Two of each kind
Makes up four.

A moment later, Hermia lay down as well. While the four of them slept, Puck squeezed flower juice into Lysander's eyes.

No more go ill,
Jack shall have Jill.
Now it is shown
Each takes his own.

Quietly, barely ruffling the flowers, Titania passed by. Her fairies flew after her, making a fuss of Bottom.

"Be gone!" Titania told the fairies suddenly. "My love and I must sleep."

Puck saw Titania cuddling Bottom's big donkey head and burst out laughing.

"I'm beginning to feel sorry for her," said Oberon, appearing from behind a tree. "I'm going to take off the spell. And you, Puck, must do the same for that poor donkey."

Oberon gently touched Titania's eyes and she woke with a sigh. "Come on," he said. "Let's go. Tomorrow we'll dance at Theseus's wedding and bless the happy couple."

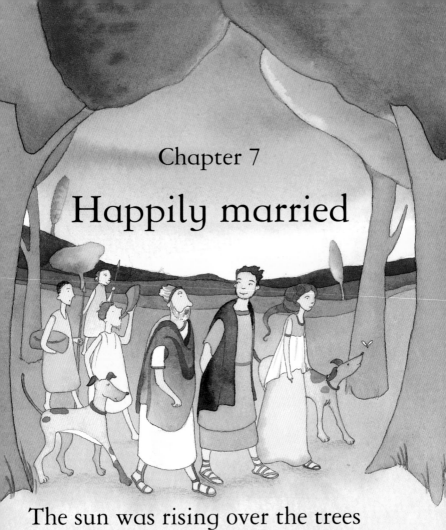

# Chapter 7

# Happily married

The sun was rising over the trees when the shrill blast of a horn shattered the forest calm. Theseus had come out hunting with Hippolyta and Egeus.

"Look who's here!" Theseus cried, noticing four stirring figures. The four quickly jumped up.

"My lord," said Lysander, bowing to the Duke.

Theseus looked at Lysander, and then at Demetrius. "I thought you both wanted to marry the same girl. What happened?"

Lysander shrugged. "I've no idea. Hermia and I were running away..."

"What?" burst out Egeus, with a scowl on his face. "Outrageous! Clap him in irons. Demetrius, you nearly lost your wife."

"Ah," said Demetrius. "About that... It's a funny thing, but my love for Hermia has melted like snow. It's Helena I adore."

You're all crazy!

Egeus turned purple with rage, but Theseus smiled. "Excellent!" he said. "We can all be married together." Taking Hippolyta's hand, he led the happy couples back to his palace.

No one noticed Bottom waking up. "What an amazing dream," he mumbled, as he too left the woods. "I thought I was a donkey!"

A few hours later, three weddings had taken place. Theseus's palace was packed with guests, settling back to enjoy the sad tale of Pyramus and Thisbe.

Here are the actors – and here is our show!

To a trumpet fanfare, Bottom, Flute and Snout walked around the stage. Snout stood in the middle as the wall, and the play began.

"This is no good," said Bottom, as Pyramus. "Let's meet in the graveyard." Flute nodded and all three trooped off.

As they left, Snug crawled in with Starveling, who was carrying a hoop of lights. Snug gave a roar.

I'm a fierce lion, but don't be scared. It's only pretend!

See my lights? I'm the Moon.

Flute came on again, tripping over his dress. "Where are you, Pyramus, my love?" he called.

Snug roared and Flute ran away, screaming. As he fled, his scarf fell off. Snug chewed it greedily.

61

Bottom came back and snatched up the scarf. "Thisbe? Eaten by a lion?" he sobbed. "My dainty duck is no more." Turning to face the audience, he pulled out a fake dagger and stabbed himself.

With a cry of despair, Flute rushed on and pretended to die too. As his body fell on Bottom, the audience clapped and cheered.

Unseen above, the fairy king and
queen were also watching the play.
Puck flew over the room, sprinkling
everyone with fairy dust. Oberon
smiled. "Now they'll all live
happily ever after," he said.
And they did.

William Shakespeare (1564-1616) was born in Stratford-upon-Avon, England, but became famous as an actor and writer when he moved to London. He wrote numerous poems and almost forty plays which are still performed and enjoyed today.

### Internet links

For links to websites where you can read more about Shakespeare, go to the Usborne Quicklinks Website at **www.usborne-quicklinks.com** and type the keywords **YR Shakespeare**. Please note that Usborne Publishing cannot be responsible for the content of any website other than its own.

Designed by Natacha Goransky
Cover design: Russell Punter

First published in 2005 by Usborne Publishing Ltd., Usborne House, 83-85 Saffron Hill, London EC1N 8RT, England. www.usborne.com